THE TRIAL OF SACCO AND VANZETTI

A Primary Source Account

Kerry Hinton

rosen central
Primary Source™
The Rosen Publishing Group, Inc., New York

Published in 2004 by The Rosen Publishing Group, Inc.
29 East 21st Street, New York, NY 10010

Unless otherwise attributed, all quotes in this book are excerpted from court transcripts.

First Edition

Library of Congress Cataloging-in-Publication Data

Hinton, Kerry.
The trial of Sacco and Vanzetti: a primary source account/by Kerry Hinton.—1st ed.
    v. cm.—(Great trials of the twentieth century)
Includes bibliographical references and index.
Contents: Humble beginnings—Two crimes—Setting a trap—The first trial: Plymouth, Massachusetts—The second trial: Dedham, Massachusetts—The long road: 1921–1927—Sacco, Vanzetti, and history.
ISBN 0-8239-3973-1 (library binding)
1. Sacco, Nicola, 1891–1927—Trials, litigation, etc.—Juvenile literature.
2. Vanzetti, Bartolomeo, 1888–1927—Trials, litigation, etc.—Juvenile literature.
3. Trials (Murder)—Massachusetts—Juvenile literature. [1. Sacco, Nicola, 1891–1927—Trials, litigation, etc. 2. Vanzetti, Bartolomeo, 1888–1927—Trials, litigation, etc. 3. Trials (Murder)]
I. Title. II. Series: Great trials of the 20th century.

KF224.S2H56 2003
345.73'02523'09744—dc21

                                                                        2002153699

Manufactured in the United States of America

CONTENTS

After the verdict of the Sacco and Vanzetti trial was announced, thousands of people in the United States and around the world protested the way the case had been handled. This photograph shows a demonstration of 12,000 workers gathering in New York City's Union Square on August 9, 1927, in support of the convicted immigrants.

INTRODUCTION

On April 15, 1920, in South Braintree, Massachusetts, a paymaster and a guard for a shoe factory were robbed and shot to death in broad daylight. The payroll, which was never recovered, totaled nearly $16,000. Witnesses to the crime described the shooters as looking "Italian."

Within one month, local police arrested two Italian immigrants named Nicola Sacco and Bartolomeo Vanzetti. Both men were known anarchists, both were armed, and both lied to the police upon their arrest. All of this made them suspicious in the eyes of authorities.

When the men stood trial, these factors severely influenced the prosecution and the jury against them. In addition, Sacco and Vanzetti had the misfortune of having their trial conducted by a conservative judge who opposed widespread immigration and despised radical members of society such as socialists and anarchists. Although both men had alibis that were confirmed by multiple witnesses, they were found guilty of murder and sentenced to death.

There was international uproar and concern following the trial. Well-known activists, authors, actors, and political figures joined one another in protest of what many people saw to be an incredibly unfair arrest and trial procedure. Many people believed that the two men were arrested more on the basis of their race and political beliefs than any real evidence linking them to the crime.

After seven years of hearings and denied requests for appeals, Sacco and Vanzetti met their ends in separate electric chairs on August 23, 1927. Since 1977, August 23 has been officially recognized as Sacco and Vanzetti Day in the state of Massachusetts.

Thousands of people have been sentenced to death and subsequently executed in the history of the United States, but almost eighty years after Sacco and Vanzetti drew their last breaths, their case is still discussed in many American history classes and law school lecture halls around the world. What made this case so intriguing and controversial? This book will examine what made and still makes the story of these two unassuming immigrants one of the most important court cases ever to be heard in the United States.

HUMBLE BEGINNINGS

In 1908, sixteen-year-old Ferdinando Sacco (who would later change his name to Nicola) came from the south of Italy with his older brother, Sabino, who was nineteen. The brothers came to settle in Massachusetts and worked for a construction firm. In 1909, Sabino returned to Italy, leaving his brother on his own. The younger Sacco brother took lessons in shoemaking, which resulted in his employment at the Milford Shoe Factory. Sacco was so trusted at the factory that he was often asked to perform additional duties as a night watchman. As a young immigrant in the United States, he worked hard to support his wife, Rosina, and their son, Dante.

Bartolomeo Vanzetti also came to America from Italy, but from the northern part of the country. His father was a middle-class farmer who later opened a café. As a teen, young Vanzetti learned to work hard. He left school at the age of thirteen to work as a baker's apprentice. Vanzetti worked seven days a week for fifteen hours a day until he contracted pleurisy, an illness that affects the lungs. While he was recovering, Vanzetti began to read almost every book he could find relating to philosophy and religion.

Four years after coming to the United States from his native Italy, Nicola Sacco married Rosina Zambelli. In 1912, they had a son, Dante. Their daughter, Ines, was born in 1920, just months after her father's arrest for robbery and murder. Taken circa 1915, this photograph shows Sacco with Dante and Rosina in Massachusetts. This is the picture Sacco said he gave the Italian consul on the day of the South Braintree murder.

Like the Sacco brothers, Vanzetti came to the United States in 1908. For five grueling months, Vanzetti was unable to find work in New York and found himself homeless and sleeping on the streets. Sometime in 1913, he traveled north to Springfield, Massachusetts, where he obtained a job in construction. He settled in Plymouth and boarded with another family of Italian émigrés, the Brinis.

ENTER THE ANARCHISTS

Sacco and Vanzetti met thanks to their involvement with the anarchist movement. Anarchism is the theory that supports the idea that any form of dominant government is wrong, due to the belief that any degree of power is bound to corrupt. Some of the guiding principles that make up the foundation of anarchy are brotherhood and self-government. During the early 1900s, anarchists supported

Bartolomeo Vanzetti, pictured here in a Massachusetts courthouse in 1921, was deeply committed to his cause. He often referred to a quote by Saint Augustine that he had memorized as a child, "The blood of martyrs is the seed of liberty."

causes of the common man, such as workers' rights and the fight against discrimination.

Sacco's first involvement with radical politics occurred in 1912, when he assisted in the defense of another Italian immigrant whom he believed to be unjustly accused of murder. Within a year's time, Sacco was attending regular meetings of a local anarchist group called Circolo di

OUR STATUE OF LIBERTY. — SHE CAN STAND IT.

Studi Sociali (Social Studies Circle). After taking part in a worker's strike the following year, Sacco fully embraced the anarchists and their cause.

During this time, Sacco was exposed to the writings of Luigi Galleani, which would have a strong effect on his beliefs for the rest of his life. Vanzetti also involved himself during these years in protests, writing, and supporting striking workers who demanded better wages and working conditions.

It is important to understand that the ideas of anarchy and political resistance did not enter into the lives of Sacco or Vanzetti until they had lived in the United States for a few years. The poor working and living conditions faced at this time by laborers and newly arrived immigrants led both men to conclude that life would be improved if people were allowed to govern themselves. They believed this could only happen without the presence of a dominant government. As their experiences further opened their eyes, Sacco and Vanzetti grew increasingly dissatisfied with any organizations or policies that prevented men and women from having better jobs and lives.

The story of Sacco and Vanzetti cannot be accurately told without the presence of their ties to anarchism. As Vanzetti wrote in his autobiography, *The Story of a Proletarian Life*,

> "I am and will be until the last instant (unless I should discover that I am in error) an anarchist communist, because I believe that communism is the most humane form of social contract, because I know that only with liberty can man rise, become noble, and complete."

Illustrated by artist C. J. Taylor, this political cartoon, entitled, "Our Statue of Liberty—She Can Stand It," was created on October 27, 1886. The cartoon shows representations of anarchism, socialism, georgeism, boycott, communism, and intolerance trying to bring down the symbolic statue with ropes and dynamite. As the United States received greater numbers of immigrants from a wider variety of nations, citizens feared that the different political ideas that came along with them would threaten the foundation of their country.

ANARCHISM

A narchism (Greek for "having no ruler") is a school of thought that strives to banish any form of dominance over any group of people. The goal of anarchists is to have a system in which people can make decisions for themselves. Without the state or ruling government, anarchists believe that the better parts of human nature will take over. This will allow people to live together and cooperate with the freedom of self-rule instead of the burden of laws.

Today, the word "anarchism" has taken on a negative meaning, partly because of acts of terrorism committed by some anarchists in the early part of the twentieth century. In theory, however, the goals of anarchy are very noble. They include freedom from racism, starvation, poverty, and pain.

Since they lived in different towns, the two men did not meet each other until May 1917 at an anarchist meeting in Boston. One week later they fled to Mexico with other Italian American anarchists to avoid being drafted to fight for the United States in World War I. Neither Sacco nor Vanzetti believed he had any cause to bear arms against anyone in the conflict. This departure would come to haunt the two men when they went to trial in 1921. Their dodging of the draft was seen as proof that both men were extremely disloyal to the United States in thought and action.

Sacco and Vanzetti returned to the United States in September 1917. Sacco moved with his family to Stoughton, Massachusetts, and continued to work in the shoe industry. Vanzetti settled in nearby Plymouth to work as a fishmonger.

TWO CRIMES

The trial of Sacco and Vanzetti hinges on two separate criminal acts, one harmless and the other deadly. The first—the crime that formed the foundation of the case against Sacco and Vanzetti—took place in the quiet little town of Bridgewater, Massachusetts. On December 24, 1919, four men attempted to steal the payroll of a shoe company. The robbery was unsuccessful, however, and the holdup men fled the scene without stealing anything or harming anyone. Witnesses could only describe the robbers as "dark." Bridgewater's chief of police, Michael Stewart, suspected radicals who needed to steal the money to fund their cause, but he was unsuccessful in finding any leads to investigate.

SOUTH BRAINTREE

Less than four months later, a similar robbery was attempted in South Braintree, Massachusetts. On April 15, 1920, Frederick A. Parmenter, a paymaster for the Slater and Morrill shoe factory, was

The photograph on the top shows the Slater and Morrill shoe factory, whose paymaster and guard were murdered. The site of the robbery and murder was just past the Rice and Hutchins shoe factory *(bottom)* on Pearl Street, in South Braintree, Massachusetts. During the Sacco and Vanzetti trial, an eyewitness identified Nicola Sacco by saying, "Well, I wouldn't say it was [Sacco], but he is a dead image of him."

Sacco's .32 caliber Colt automatic *(top)* and Vanzetti's .38 caliber Harrington & Richardson *(bottom)* were used as evidence. Vanzetti's gun was a concern because it resembled the weapon carried by the paymaster Berardelli. Tests conducted in 1977 revealed that Berardelli's gun had actually been .32 caliber.

transporting about $16,000 of employee pay from one building to another. Alessandro Berardelli, an armed guard hired to protect the company payroll, accompanied him.

A small construction crew was doing excavation work across the street from Parmenter's destination. Parked by the main building was a car that eyewitnesses later described as a "strange Buick." Two men dressed in dark clothing appeared to be performing repairs on the vehicle. As Parmenter and Berardelli walked toward the building, they passed two other men dressed in dark clothes. One of the men approached Berardelli, and gunshots soon followed.

The sound of the gunshots created a panic. The workers across the street scattered. Berardelli had been shot and was crying out for help from his position on the ground. Parmenter dropped the money box he was carrying and began to run at the sound of the first gunshot. As he fled, one of the men shot him in the back. Parmenter crossed the street and collapsed.

A third armed burglar arrived at about this time and began to fire shots at Berardelli. One of the two original gunmen crossed Pearl Street and fired at Parmenter again to make sure he was dead. The Buick moved closer to the crime scene, and the three gunmen joined the two men who had been waiting with the car earlier. One of the

LUIGI GALLEANI

Luigi Galleani was the best-known Italian anarchist of the twentieth century. He moved to the United States in 1901 along with many other Italians to escape the rapidly worsening financial conditions in Italy. In 1903, Galleani began to publish a newspaper called *Cronaca Sovversiva* (*Subversive Chronicle*), for which Sacco and Vanzetti both eventually worked.

Like many anarchists, Galleani favored swift and rapid changes in the government to improve everyday life for everyone. However, he sought to achieve this change by any means, including terrorism and assassination. Galleani's followers, known as Galleanists, began to acquire a reputation for violence. This image was never fully separated from the anarchist movement and ultimately led to its virtual disappearance in the 1930s.

Galleanists were responsible for most of the bombings aimed at political figures opposed to the anarchist cause between 1910 and 1920. One of the most deadly of these bombings occurred on Wall Street in New York City in 1920. The bombing was planned by Mike Boda, a comrade of Sacco and Vanzetti who reportedly committed the act in retaliation for the arrests of Sacco and Vanzetti.

Galleani was deported to Italy in 1919, a year before the arrest of Sacco and Vanzetti. The Italian government of Mussolini was Fascist and opposed to the goals of anarchists. Galleani was jailed many times after he returned to Italy and spent the last few years of his life living on a small island off the Italian coast. He died of a heart attack in November 1931, four years after the executions of Sacco and Vanzetti.

gunmen picked up the money box on his way into the car. Berardelli was bleeding heavily and was moved inside a nearby house, where he died soon after. Parmenter was taken to a local hospital and died twelve hours later.

As the getaway car drove through South Braintree and beyond, it was spotted by seven witnesses. All of the witnesses noted similar features of the strange car, including its size, a torn window curtain that fluttered as the car bounced along bumpy roads, and a rifle sticking out of the rear window. Many witnesses also took note of the men and their dark clothing, which they reported to the local police. The last sighting of the Buick was in a small town about twenty miles from South Braintree.

THE INVESTIGATION

Initially, local police had very few leads to help them solve the brutal killings in South Braintree. Officials began to think that some of the men from the attempted robbery in Bridgewater might have been involved in the crimes in South Braintree.

The day Parmenter and Berardelli were killed in South Braintree, an Italian immigrant named Ferruccio Coacci was to be deported to his native country. Coacci, like his comrade Sacco, worked in a shoe factory in Bridgewater and had been forced to leave the United States because of his involvement with *Cronaca Sovversiva*, the anarchist paper published by the now-deported Luigi Galleani. However, Coacci never reported to the Bureau of Immigration to leave the United States. Coacci told an immigration officer that his wife was extremely ill and he needed to care for her. The Bureau of Immigration found Coacci's story suspicious and contacted Michael Stewart, police chief of Bridgewater, to investigate.

Chief Stewart dispatched two officers to Coacci's home. When the two men arrived at the Coacci residence, they were very surprised to find Mrs. Coacci healthy and alert. To make the apparent lie told by Coacci even stranger, the two investigators found him hurriedly packing his bags and asking the officers to deport him as soon as possible. Within a few days, Coacci was on his way to Italy.

Mortal Bullet Ex. 18   Lowell Test Bullets.

This photograph shows Bullet 3 (exhibit 18), which killed Berardelli, positioned in a side-by-side comparison with a bullet fired from Nicola Sacco's gun. Ballistics experts testified that the mortal bullet's rifling marks (the grooves made in bullets as a result of its journey through the gun's barrel) matched those on the test bullet fired from Sacco's gun. The jury later commented that this evidence was compelling enough for them to convict Sacco.

Two days after the visit to the Coacci household, the "strange Buick" seen by many witnesses on the day of the robbery was found a few miles from Coacci's home. Tracks indicating the presence of another car were spotted leading away from the Buick. Stewart began to suspect that Coacci was involved in the horrible crimes of South Braintree. Finding the Buick was important to the police, but they also needed to know where the other car was and who had driven it.

Stewart and the police returned to Coacci's house a few days later to investigate a possible connection to the Buick found so close to his residence. While there, Stewart interviewed a boarder and friend of Coacci's named Mike Boda. Like Sacco and Vanzetti, Boda was an Italian immigrant with anarchist leanings. Boda told the police he was a salesman and that he owned a car that was being repaired at a local garage.

Using statements from witnesses, Stewart believed he was looking for an Italian man who drove or owned a car in the vicinity of Cochesett, which was twenty miles south of South Braintree. Coupled with his anarchist association, Mike Boda was beginning to fit the description the authorities had in mind.

Stewart began to believe that both Coacci and Boda were involved in the South Braintree crime. According to all eyewitness reports, five men worked together in the robbery, leaving Stewart in need of three more conspirators to complete his criminal quintet.

SETTING A TRAP

CHAPTER 3

During the investigation of the South Braintree robbery, Justice Department officials in Boston worked together with the law enforcement community in Bridgewater. Even though the Justice Department believed the South Braintree crime had been committed by professionals, Stewart continued to pursue the known associates of Boda and Coacci, partly due to their status as "radicals to be watched." Stewart contacted the local garage and instructed the owner to notify him if Boda or anyone else came to pick up the car.

Anarchists everywhere were very concerned for their freedom and safety during this time. The United States was at the height of the Red Scare (see page 26), and the antiradical sentiments throughout the country made life difficult for anarchists as well as other fringe groups. In 1919, at May Day parades for workers' rights in Boston, Cleveland, and New York, riots had broken out. That same year, bombs were detonated throughout the country at the homes of many key antiradical figures, including U. S. Attorney General A. Mitchell Palmer. J. Edgar Hoover, who would later head the Federal Bureau of

This photograph, taken on September 16, 1920, in New York City, shows the aftermath of the explosion by the bomb set off in protest of the Sacco and Vanzetti situation. Many newspapers across the country blamed the bombing on Luigi Galleani, without having any proof. *Inset:* This portrait of future FBI director J. Edgar Hoover was taken circa 1910. It became Hoover's responsibility to help Attorney General Palmer rid the nation of radicals.

Investigation (FBI), was appointed the first chief of the Department of Justice's Anti-Radical Division. The bombing campaign undertaken by some of the anarchists who chose not to go underground had continued despite the Palmer Raids that were instituted to purge radical individuals, groups, and publications from America. It was increasingly common for many people with radical views to be detained and questioned with very little basis or proof of wrongdoing.

One of these detainees was Andrea Salsedo, who had worked for *Cronaca Sovversiva* and was suspected of involvement in at least one of the bombings. Salsedo and Roberto Elia, another *Cronaca* supporter and worker, were apprehended by the Department of Justice without any cause or proof in March 1920, one month before the South Braintree robbery. Two months later, Salsedo was still in custody and had not been allowed to have any contact with the outside world. Salsedo had been beaten repeatedly and died on May 3, 1920, when he fell to his death from the fourteenth-floor window of the building in which he was held. To this day, opinions vary on how Salsedo fell. Some believe he jumped out of guilt for his anarchist misdeeds, while some theorize that

U.S. Attorney General A. Mitchell Palmer was photographed in the Supreme Court in 1920. Palmer's hatred and fear of radicals is evident in his famous 1920 essay, "The Case Against the Reds." "Like a prairie-fire," he wrote, "the blaze of revolution was sweeping over every American institution of law and order . . . It was eating its way into the homes of the American workmen."

he was thrown from the window to serve as an example for other radicals who may have been planning terrorist acts.

No matter what caused Salsedo's fall, his death caused a great deal of fear in anarchist circles. Attorney General A. Mitchell Palmer announced that prior to his death Salsedo had given crucial information regarding the bomb plot of a year before in which the

Nicola Sacco *(left)* and Bartolomeo Vanzetti *(right)* were committed anarchists who believed that government rule inhibited the best parts of human nature, therefore encouraging evils such as racism and poverty. Along with other anarchists, they moved to Mexico during World War I so they wouldn't have to fight for the United States. In Mexico, Sacco adopted the pseudonym he would use for the rest of his life, Nicola.

homes of many antiradical government figures had been destroyed. This news made many anarchists decide to quiet their activities. It is possible that Sacco and Vanzetti made this same choice when they found out about the loss of their comrade on May 4.

THE ARREST

Sacco and Vanzetti took a streetcar to the Elm Square Garage in West Bridgewater on the evening of May 5 to meet Mike Boda and another friend, Riccardo Orciani. The men planned to retrieve Boda's repaired car and remove any documents that could link them to Salsedo, bombing plots, or the anarchist cause.

The men found the garage locked and went to the home of its owner, Simon Johnson, to retrieve the car. Chief Stewart had left instructions to call him if anyone came to pick up Boda's car. When the four men knocked on Johnson's door, Johnson's wife called the police. Johnson suggested to Boda that he not take the car, primarily because it had no license plates. Boda and Orciani rode away on a motorcycle. Sacco and Vanzetti walked back to the streetcar and boarded it to go to Sacco's house.

The police boarded the streetcar at one of its regular stops and arrested the two men as "suspicious characters." The arresting officers claimed that the two men reached into their coats, as if to draw guns.

As soon as Sacco and Vanzetti were arrested, events began to spiral out of control to almost condemn them before they were even legitimately charged with a crime. The police found anarchist leaflets on the men. More important, Sacco and Vanzetti were both armed with handguns and had bullets for these guns in their pockets.

From this point on, matters continued to worsen for the two men. In police captivity, each man was questioned separately, and each gave different answers for the same questions. Neither of the two men's reasons for being armed seemed believable to the police. Sacco and Vanzetti also denied knowing Boda and Orciani several times, which the police knew to be false.

Why would Sacco and Vanzetti lie to the police? Many argued during and after their trial that the initial falsehoods proved that they were

THE RED SCARE (1919–1920)

After World War I, a rise in antiradical thought and policy occurred. The United States government was very wary of individuals and groups who did not support the war effort in Europe. The government began to suppress speakers and publications whose views they considered extreme. This period came to be known as the Red Scare. The "reds" represented the Bolshevik Communists who overthrew the Russian monarchy in 1917 and withdrew their troops from the battlefields of World War I.

Those who did not support fighting in the war, including some members of labor unions, college professors, socialists, communists, and anarchists, were under suspicion and were watched carefully. Many of these people were detained or arrested under the authority of federal laws that were designed to limit the rights of these "unpatriotic" individuals. The victims of these raids (known as Palmer Raids, after Attorney General A. Mitchell Palmer) and arrests were often denied the right to obtain a lawyer or defend themselves, and many were swiftly deported.

Laws limiting personal freedoms were also passed during this time. One of these laws was the Sedition Act of May 1918, which was passed by President Woodrow Wilson. This act made criticizing the government and its policies illegal and punishable by fines or imprisonment. This was a huge blow to the civil liberties of all United States citizens.

These two years of anticommunist hysteria had a direct and profound effect on Sacco and Vanzetti, who had the misfortune to be arrested during the height of the Red Scare. Their political views and immigrant status only worsened the public's perception of them as they went to trial.

guilty of the South Braintree robbery. The fact that they were armed seems to support this idea for some, demonstrating what Chief Stewart and others called a "consciousness of guilt." This means that he believed since Sacco and Vanzetti were acting suspicious and were not entirely honest, they had to be guilty.

On the other hand, it is important to remember that Sacco and Vanzetti were anarchists in a time when being an anarchist was extremely dangerous. At the time of their arrest, the two men were not charged with any specific crime. Without being informed of a charge, Sacco and Vanzetti most likely assumed they were being held because they were radicals. Lying to the police may have seemed like their best defense.

THE FIRST TRIAL: PLYMOUTH, MASSACHUSETTS

Sacco and Vanzetti represented a fraction of the five-man "gang" whom Bridgewater chief of police Stewart hoped to bring to justice. Riccardo Orciani had a solid alibi for his whereabouts on the days of the robberies at Bridgewater and South Braintree, and he was let go. Mike Boda left the country. Stewart was left with two-fifths of his crime team and decided to put them on trial.

Sacco and Vanzetti were charged with murder on May 5, 1920, in connection with the crimes of South Braintree, but they were not indicted until September. Based on an eyewitness who believed Vanzetti was the driver of the truck seen at Bridgewater, the district attorney decided to indict Vanzetti alone on June 11 for the botched robbery attempt of December 1919. The state was unable to indict Sacco, who had witnesses to verify that he was in Boston with his wife having pictures taken.

The trial for the Bridgewater robbery attempt began on June 22, 1920, in Plymouth, Massachusetts. Presiding over Vanzetti's first trial was an individual who would forever be linked to the fates of Sacco and

Judge Webster Thayer was seen by many to have acted unfairly and with great prejudice in the Sacco and Vanzetti trial. His conduct, however, impressed the jurors. In his charge to the jury, Thayer said, "I therefore beseech you not to allow the fact that the defendants are Italians to influence or prejudice you in the least degree. They are entitled, under the law, to the same rights and consideration as though their ancestors came over in the *Mayflower*."

Vanzetti—Judge Webster Thayer. Thayer was a conservative judge and member of the upper class who believed that anyone who held anarchist or radical beliefs was not only a threat to liberty but also an "accessory to murder before the fact."

From the outset of the Bridgewater robbery trial, the fact that Vanzetti was an immigrant seemed to have a negative effect on the proceedings. For example, one of the witnesses for the prosecution stated that he could tell one of the criminals was a foreigner by "the way he ran." Accounts like this only worsened the jury's impression of Vanzetti.

More than twenty witnesses for the defense verified Vanzetti's alibi, which was that he had been selling eels in Plymouth on the morning in question. Still, this was not enough to acquit Vanzetti of the Bridgewater attempt. Many of the witnesses were lower- to middle-class Italian immigrants who could not speak English fluently. Their

This political cartoon was drawn by Fred Ellis and published in the *Daily Worker* in 1927. It accuses the United States of hypocrisy using the symbol of freedom, the Statue of Liberty. This time, an electric chair sits atop the pedestal, a vulture perched on the backrest. The cartoon suggests that Americans were hungry vultures waiting for the death of the new wave of immigrants, who were not as welcome as the Statue of Liberty would suggest.

testimonies were given through a translator, which probably was less convincing to an English-speaking jury.

The arrangement of Massachusetts's courtrooms during this time did nothing to hold up the idea of "innocent until proven guilty." Defendants were forced to sit in the middle of the courtroom on a wrought-iron bench that had raised sides, making it resemble a cage. Although this was customary at the time, factors like this may have made it even more difficult for a jury to reach a completely honest and unbiased decision regarding accused individuals.

Vanzetti chose not to take the stand to testify on his own behalf, which also severely hurt his case. His reluctance to speak in court might have caused him to appear guilty. In reality, Vanzetti did not take the stand because he was most likely fearful that his radical activities would be revealed. Such information could convince the jury that he was an Italian immigrant and anarchist who was therefore guilty of a failed robbery attempt.

None of these things was individually damning, but all were factors that could have influenced a jury that Vanzetti was guilty, even without proper proof to convict him.

When a verdict was reached, Vanzetti was found guilty of assault with intent to rob and assault with intent to murder. Judge Thayer sentenced him to twelve to fifteen years in prison. This was an unusually harsh sentence for a crime in which no one was injured.

It was more than likely that Sacco and Vanzetti were going to trial for the South Braintree murders. This time, Vanzetti would go before a jury as a convicted felon. The prosecutors believed that Vanzetti's conviction for the Bridgewater robbery attempt would help make the two men appear even guiltier when they stood trial for the robbery and murders in South Braintree.

THE SECOND TRIAL: DEDHAM, MASSACHUSETTS

O n May 6, 1920, one day after the arrest of Sacco and Vanzetti, friends and supporters of the two men formed the Sacco-Vanzetti Defense Committee. The mission of this group was to raise money for the legal defense of "the eel-seller" (Vanzetti) and "the shoe-edger" (Sacco).

Sacco and Vanzetti retained the services of attorney Fred H. Moore, who had gained notice defending other radical clients. Moore intended to show the jury that the prosecution was more concerned with trying Sacco and Vanzetti for their anarchist beliefs and immigrant status than the actual crimes.

To counteract the allegations of the prosecution, Moore decided to have Sacco and Vanzetti admit to their beliefs in the courtroom. He hoped that this would reveal to the jury that the two men were not arrested because they were thought to have murdered Parmenter and Berardelli in South Braintree but because they were immigrant radicals. Moore wanted to convince the jury that Sacco and Vanzetti happened to be in the wrong place at the wrong time. Moore also wanted to show

On October 31, 1921, as shown in this photograph, members of the riot squad of the Boston Police Department guarded the Norfolk County Courthouse in Dedham, Massachusetts, where the Sacco and Vanzetti trial was held. Security was called to the scene to prevent rioting, which was expected from the many passionate supporters of the two accused immigrants. In the week before, an attempt was made by protesters to bomb the American Embassy in Paris, and violent outbreaks had occurred elsewhere around the world.

the jury and court that Sacco and Vanzetti were only two men who represented part of a much larger organization that was a known target of the federal government: the Italian anarchists.

Moore was also very active outside the courtroom. Through his efforts, Sacco and Vanzetti received more and more attention nation-wide as the case continued. During the course of the trial, Moore contacted local newspapers and even Boston papers, and made sure

Fred Moore was the first counsel for Sacco and Vanzetti. This portrait was taken in 1927, after he had earned more than $100,000 for his work on the case. A Californian known for his defense of radicals, Moore was not familiar with Massachusetts law and was not liked by Sacco's wife. In addition, he was reported to have been a cocaine addict and needed to be supplied with the drug throughout the trial.

articles were written about the trial to put his clients in a sympathetic light. By the time Sacco and Vanzetti's trial concluded on July 14, 1921, they would find themselves to be two of the most discussed men on the face of the earth.

THE PROSECUTION'S CASE

The odds continued to go against Sacco and Vanzetti as court proceedings progressed in Dedham, Massachusetts. The jury was hardly unbiased. None of the jurors were

The document above is a fund-raising petition created by the Sacco-Vanzetti Defense Committee in Boston, Massachusetts, in 1921. In order to pay for legal expenses, fund-raising letters were sent out and volunteers took to the streets with petitions like this.

Italian, and very few were immigrants. Walter R. Ripley, the foreman of the jury, was heard to say, "They ought to hang them anyway!" when asked if Sacco and Vanzetti were innocent or guilty.

The trial began on May 31, 1921, with Judge Webster Thayer presiding once again. Some historians believe that Thayer specifically asked for this case. This unfortunate assignment seemed to favor District Attorney Frederick Katzmann, who was continually allowed to bring up the political affiliations and beliefs of the two accused men. Despite constant objections, Thayer chose to let Katzmann make these statements. This worked against Sacco and Vanzetti because it colored the jury's view of the defendants and shifted focus from the crimes to the moral character of the two men.

In this 1927 photograph, Herbert Ehrmann and William Thompson are leaving the Boston statehouse after meeting with Governor Alvan T. Fuller about the Sacco and Vanzetti case. Thompson stepped in to defend the two men during the lengthy appeals process. Thompson was a prominent Boston attorney and knew the Massachusetts laws. He argued the post-trial motions before the state supreme court in 1926.

Both the prosecution's and defense's cases began and ended with the testimony of eyewitnesses. Unfortunately for the defense, the Commonwealth of Massachusetts also had material evidence to present to the jury. Despite the fact that some of this evidence was suspect and vague, it was more convincing than Sacco and Vanzetti's defense, which relied solely on proving their whereabouts on the day of the South Braintree robbery and murders. Sacco and Vanzetti's alibis could only be proven by eyewitnesses, not with physical objects.

Part of the prosecution's case also concerned items that were outside the scope of the evidence alone. Judge Thayer was very conservative and was not fond of Fred H. Moore, Sacco and Vanzetti's attorney, because of Moore's history of providing legal aid and assistance to radical groups. Moore was from the western United States, not Massachusetts, and was viewed as an outsider by Thayer and the prosecution. In his summation, or closing statement, Moore noted to the court that he felt as if he were "all alien."

Sacco and Vanzetti may have been accused of working together on the same crime, but their roles were seen to be very different by the prosecution. In fact, the Commonwealth of Massachusetts had more evidence linking Sacco to the murders than Vanzetti. The prosecution developed the theory that Sacco was one of the gunmen, while Vanzetti sat in the car waiting to assist if necessary.

The prosecution's case against Sacco and Vanzetti hinged on three major points:

1. Sacco and Vanzetti were the members of a robbery "gang." Vanzetti aided Sacco, who was one of the men to fire a gun at the scene of the crime.

2. The prosecution had a bullet from the crime scene that was fired by Sacco. This bullet killed Berardelli.

3. The lies Sacco and Vanzetti told the police on the evening of their arrests showed "consciousness of guilt," which meant they were acting guilty because they were guilty.

To prove these points, District Attorney Katzmann used three main strategies: eyewitness testimonies, ballistics, and the alibis of the two men on the day of the crime.

EYEWITNESSES TO THE CRIME

By the trial's end, many agreed that the eyewitness accounts were at best very vague. Suspiciously, many of the eyewitnesses called by District Attorney Katzmann "remembered" additional details more than a year after the crime than they had stated originally to police just after the murders. When the prosecution rested its case, five eye-witnesses confidently placed Sacco in the car or at the crime scene. The prosecution's star witness, Mary Splaine, saw the man she believed to be Sacco for less than three seconds from the second-floor window of the Slater and Morrill shoe factory. Additionally, her identification at the trial was much more detailed than the report she had given to private investigators a year earlier.

Another woman, Lola Andrews, testified that she had spoken to a man performing repairs on a car outside the shoe factory on the day of the robbery. Although she identified Sacco as the man at the trial, she had been unable to identify him when shown his picture soon after the robbery occurred. When the defense asked her if this were true, she said no. Even though this testimony was not completely true, neither Judge Thayer nor the prosecution investigated further. At least three witnesses called by the prosecution had their testimony contradicted by the testimony of other witnesses.

The prosecution tried to link Sacco to a cap found at the crime scene. The cap resembled the one that Sacco normally wore, according to a witness. It also had a small hole worn into it, which the prosecutors argued was caused by the hook Sacco used to hang his cap on at the shoe factory. The defense argued that the cap could have belonged to anyone—witnesses or even passing onlookers who arrived after the crime. The cap was entered as evidence. Sacco denied owning the cap. When he tried it on, it did not fit. It also had earflaps, which Sacco said his cap did not have.

Eyewitnesses to the Braintree crime testified they saw a dark Buick speeding down Pearl Street. The men inside reportedly threw nails onto the road to flatten the tires of anyone who might go after them. Believing the car to also have been used in the Bridgewater attempt, police were led to Mike Boda and then to Sacco and Vanzetti. Judge Thayer did not find evidence surrounding the automobile compelling when trying the case.

There were no witnesses who could testify without doubt that they had seen Vanzetti at the crime scene. However, four witnesses placed him near the crime scene, that is, in the town of South Braintree late in the morning of the robbery and murders. The railroad gate-tender at whom a gun had been pointed on the afternoon of the crime claimed to have seen Vanzetti get out of a car near Bridgewater on the afternoon of the crime. Other witnesses claimed to see a man who resembled Vanzetti pass by in a dark car on the same day. In attempt to counter these witnesses, the defense called thirty-one witnesses who said they did not see Vanzetti in the strange dark car used in the robbery.

BALLISTICS

Ballistics is the science of the firing, flight, and effects of ammunition. In other words, ballistics experts take a look at what bullets do on their journey from the barrel of a gun to their target. The use of ballistics in courtrooms is very important. No two guns will fire the same type of bullet the same way, and results obtained by ballistics experts are often considered unquestionable in courts of law.

The police compared the ammunition Sacco and Vanzetti had with them at the time of their arrests to the bullets taken from the bodies of the victims and the surrounding crime scene. When the two men were initially arrested, Sacco was carrying a Colt .32, and Vanzetti had a Harrington & Richardson .38 revolver.

Berardelli, the payroll guard, had been shot six times. Every ballistics expert interviewed said that five of the bullets could not have come from Sacco's gun. The bullet that caused a stir was the bullet designated "Bullet 3" for the purpose of cataloging evidence. Bullet 3 was examined, and it was determined that it could have been shot from a Colt .32, which was the same type of gun found on Sacco. One of the experts the prosecution called, Captain William H. Proctor, said that in his opinion, Bullet 3 was fired from a Colt .32, but he was never asked if he believed it had been fired from Sacco's particular pistol. The expert meant that Bullet 3 simply could have fit in Sacco's gun. He did not offer proof that the bullet was in fact fired by Sacco's gun.

Before the trial began, Captain Proctor told District Attorney Katzmann that there was no real evidence that indicated that Sacco fired Bullet 3 from his gun. Two years later, he submitted a statement saying that if he had been asked directly, he would have said that there was no proof that Bullet 3 was fired by Sacco.

The prosecution used the fact that Sacco had been armed at the time of his arrest as hard evidence that he was a murderer. In response, the defense called experts who testified that Bullet 3 could not have been fired by Sacco, due to the markings on the bullet that were taken after it was fired. When asked why he had a gun with him, Sacco replied that he was planning to go practice shooting with Vanzetti in a wooded area on the day they were arrested. As a radical, he also carried the gun for protection.

Juries are instructed to consider evidence and testimony to determine beyond a reasonable doubt whether a defendant has committed a crime. While the ballistics evidence presented in the Sacco and Vanzetti trial was hardly conclusive, it proved to be very convincing to many members of the jury. Seward Parker, a jury member, said, "You can't depend on the witnesses. But the bullets—there was no getting around that evidence."

The ballistics evidence against Vanzetti was even weaker. The only link found was that the gun Vanzetti was carrying when he was arrested was the same make of revolver that Berardelli, the payroll guard, had been known to carry on duty. While some believed that Vanzetti had stolen Berardelli's weapon, the fact that two men owned the same gun model proved to be only a coincidence. For one, Berardelli had taken his gun to a local shop to be repaired close to a month before the robbery and murders at South Braintree and had never picked it up. An expert witness testified that Vanzetti's gun showed no signs of being repaired recently. Secondly, Vanzetti was able to prove that he purchased the gun found on him from a friend. Vanzetti said he needed a gun primarily for protection. As a fish seller, he only worked with cash and was concerned with the possibility of a holdup.

ALIBIS

Another factor in determining the guilt of Sacco and Vanzetti was their whereabouts on the day of the crimes in South Braintree. One of the jobs of the defense counsel is to locate any and all witnesses who can positively identify and place the accused at a location other than the crime scene. Fred Moore produced many witnesses to back up the alibis presented by Sacco and Vanzetti to show that they were not in South Braintree on April 15, 1920.

On the day of the crime, Sacco was not at work but instead had traveled to Boston to obtain a passport. The clerk at the Italian consulate did not remember helping Sacco that day, but that was not unusual. Seven witnesses, however, did see Sacco eating at a restaurant in Boston on the day of the robbery.

It was harder for Vanzetti to prove his whereabouts. He was self-employed and did not have to report to a supervisor. Six witnesses verified that Vanzetti was selling fish in Plymouth at the time of the robbery, which would have made it impossible for him to be twenty-five miles away in South Braintree. One of the witnesses was Mrs. Alphonse Brini, Vanzetti's onetime landlord. Mrs. Brini had also testified on behalf of Vanzetti at the Bridgewater trial months earlier. Since the witness was a close friend of Vanzetti and was Italian, the prosecution completely discredited her testimony,

This 1921 photograph shows Bartolomeo Vanzetti and Nicola Sacco waiting in the prisoners' dock in the Norfolk County Courthouse in Dedham, Massachusetts. Although many have tried to argue that the appearance of the defendants in the cage prejudiced the jury, the truth is that such practice was the norm during that time. According to Dedham historian Robert Hansen on www.courttv.com, the cage was simply a work of art and a symbol of the county's prestige.

calling her "a stock, convenient and ready witness as well as a friend of the defendant Vanzetti."

THE VERDICT

After six weeks of testimonies, the prosecution and defense gave their closing arguments. Moore attacked the identification angle of the case, stressing that even the most positive identification of Sacco and Vanzetti was, at best, very vague.

On the issue of ballistics the prosecution gave a convincing argument, despite the fact that the weapons experts called gave incomplete testimony concerning Bullet 3. District Attorney Katzmann also spoke at length about consciousness of guilt, repeating that Sacco and Vanzetti admitted their guilt in the crimes by acting suspiciously and lying on the evening of their arrest.

The jury deliberated for less than four hours. On July 14, 1921, after considering the testimonies, the evidence, and the character of the accused, the jury found Sacco and Vanzetti guilty of murder in the first degree.

THE LONG ROAD: 1921–1927

The story of Nicola Sacco and Bartolomeo Vanzetti did not end with the guilty verdict. The decision of the twelve jurors was the beginning of a six-year plea for justice. A cry of protest rang out worldwide when the news of the Dedham verdict was heard. It seemed unbelievable to many people that two hardworking men could be found guilty of such horrible deeds.

The appeal for a new trial took place on two fronts—in the streets of America and in the courtroom. In October 1921, anarchist comrades of Sacco and Vanzetti organized demonstrations all over Europe. More than 25,000 police officers and troops were needed to protect the American Embassy in Paris during a rally for the two men.

People all over the world wrote letters of protest and sent them to American consulates and embassies around the world and to government offices in the United States. Support for Sacco and Vanzetti came from all walks of life. In addition to anarchists, many creative, influential, and famous people came to the defense of the men, including physicist Albert Einstein and writer H. G. Wells.

After the announcement of the verdict sentencing Sacco and Vanzetti to death, protests broke out around the world. This 1927 photograph shows Sacco and Vanzetti supporters driving around London, England, promoting a rally to be held in Hyde Park to "Save Sacco and Vanzetti." Many people overseas, in particular, cried out that the two immigrants had received an unfair trial by the United States court system.

Even the pope spoke out against the injustices Sacco and Vanzetti faced during the Dedham trial.

In Massachusetts, with Sacco and Vanzetti imprisoned, Fred Moore made six separate motions over the next three years for a new trial. Moore knew of newly discovered evidence that could clear the names of Sacco and Vanzetti. He also supplied evidence of perjury, jury misconduct, mishandling of evidence, and manipulation of witnesses by the prosecution. He believed these were solid reasons for the court to give his clients another chance.

Moore's assistant, Eugene Lyons, later claimed that Moore would stop at nothing to clear the names of his clients, he felt so strongly about their innocence. Thus, he said, Moore framed evidence and presented questionable eyewitnesses.

During the years of the appeal process, Sacco and Vanzetti became increasingly dissatisfied with the legal assistance provided by Fred Moore. Although Moore had been instrumental in getting the word to the general public about the mistreatment and injustices endured by his clients, Sacco and Vanzetti believed he was spending the money in their defense fund too freely. In addition, Moore had Sacco committed to Bridgewater State Hospital for the Criminally Insane, after Sacco attempted suicide and was diagnosed as a paranoid schizophrenic. Sacco resented Moore for his actions and wrote a letter firing him, which ended "I would not be surprise if no Somebody will find you some morning hang on lamppost."

Sacco and Vanzetti's case went before the Massachusetts Supreme Court, and in 1926 the court upheld their convictions and refused to grant them a new trial. Shortly after this denial, some anarchists made a call for bombings in retaliation.

THE MEDEIROS MOTION

Celestino Medeiros was a thug from Massachusetts who had been arrested for armed robbery. Medeiros sent a note to the *Boston*

American admitting his guilt in the South Braintree robbery and murder and stating that Sacco and Vanzetti had absolutely no involvement in the tragic events of that day in 1920. Celestino Medeiros was a member of the Morelli gang, an outfit that had long been associated with armed robbery. Joe Morelli, the gang's leader, looked very much like Nicola Sacco by many accounts. Many of the members of the gang spoke fluent and accentless English, a characteristic that many of the eyewitnesses during the Dedham trial noted when describing the robbers.

William Thompson, Sacco and Vanzetti's new attorney, saw Medeiros's claims as their ticket to freedom. He ignored some of the differences in Medeiros's story, such as the hour the crime was committed and the container used for the payroll money. In 1926, Thompson filed the Medeiros motion.

Judge Thayer denied the motion, deciding that Medeiros's history of criminal activity made him untrustworthy. The Medeiros motion was probably the most important motion filed in defense of Sacco and Vanzetti. The denial of the Medeiros appeal was seen by some to be the end of hope in the appeals process. The Massachusetts Supreme Court upheld Judge Thayer's decision early in 1927. A few days later, Judge Thayer formally sentenced Sacco and Vanzetti to die in the electric chair.

Millions of supporters refused to let hope die, signing a petition supporting Sacco and Vanzetti intended for Massachusetts governor Alvan T. Fuller. Additionally, Vanzetti wrote the governor a letter asking for clemency. Sacco did not sign the letter, since the two men were kept in separate prisons. Governor Fuller decided to personally meet with Vanzetti to speak with him about his case and the multiple appeals.

After meeting Vanzetti, Fuller organized the Lowell Committee, headed by Harvard University president Albert Lowell, to examine the case and see if a new trial was warranted. Fuller postponed the execution for thirty days in order to examine the trial records as thoroughly

Governor Alvan T. Fuller sits in his Massachusetts office. As a teenager, Fuller was forced to quit school and support the family when his father died unexpectedly. A self-starter who became a car dealership tycoon and was a member of the House of Representatives before becoming governor, Fuller appointed an advisory committee to investigate the Sacco and Vanzetti trial.

as possible. The Lowell Committee worked for two months, reviewing key points of evidence and reinterviewing witnesses to the crimes that had occurred almost eight years earlier.

At the end of the two months, the Lowell Committee decided that the case of Sacco and Vanzetti did not need to be reheard. In the

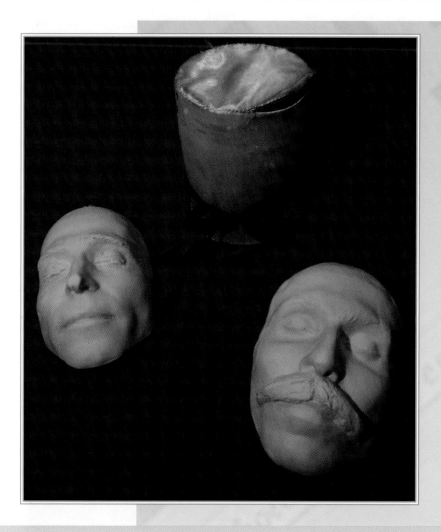

This photograph shows the death masks of Nicola Sacco *(left)* and Bartolomeo Vanzetti *(right)* and an urn containing the ashes of both men on display at a 1999 exhibit at the Boston Public Library. Before being strapped into the electric chair, Vanzetti spoke these words: "I wish to say to you that I am innocent. I have never done a crime, some sins, but never any crime. I thank you for everything you have done for me. I am innocent of all crime, not only this one, but of all, all. I am an innocent man."

eyes of the committee, Judge Thayer had presided over a fair trial. The committee's conclusion was that Sacco was guilty beyond a reasonable doubt. As for Vanzetti, they reported that they found him guilty beyond a reasonable doubt "on the whole." Governor Fuller took the advice of the Lowell Committee and decided that Sacco and Vanzetti did not deserve clemency. He set the new execution date for August 22, 1927.

Thompson made one final attempt to save the men by petitioning the U.S. Supreme Court. The appeal was never heard because the Supreme Court did not believe the trial was under their authority.

Demonstrations held throughout the world protesting the death penalty for Sacco and Vanzetti were of no help. Nicola Sacco and Bartolomeo Vanzetti were put to death by electrocution on August 23, 1927. Sacco's last words were, "Long live anarchy!"

SACCO, VANZETTI, AND HISTORY

Two unassuming and hardworking men may have died by electrocution in 1927, but their spirits live on and continue to inspire people around the world to this day. The Lowell Committee decision only increased public outrage at the conduct of the trial and subsequent appeal motions. Sacco and Vanzetti brought more attention to the idea of anarchy and radical politics than they could ever have done if they had not been arrested. The two men noted this in a joint letter written to the Sacco and Vanzetti Defense Committee two days before their deaths: "Only two of us will die. Our ideal, you our comrades, will live by millions; we have won, but not vanquished. Just treasure our suffering, our sorrow, our mistakes, our defeats, our passion for future battles and for the great emancipation."

Unfortunately, the "great emancipation," or the realization of their dreams of equality and brotherhood, never came to be. America's government now seemed to some to be as unjust as some systems of government people in other countries were trying to escape. Americans who did not see the case as unjust became more

The bodies of Sacco and Vanzetti were driven through the streets of Boston to the Joseph Langone funeral parlor at 383 Hanover Street, as shown in this photograph from August 26, 1927. Crowds of people swarmed the hearse as it traveled. Around the world, protesters rioted at American embassies and destroyed anything and everything American, such as American cars, American products, and theaters showing American films.

fearful and suspicious of immigrants from southern Europe. In 1932, five years after the deaths of Sacco and Vanzetti, Judge Thayer's house was bombed. No one was ever charged in connection with the crime.

Writers, artists, and poets attempted to make sense of the trial and executions. Artist Ben Shahn painted a famous piece entitled *The Passion of Sacco and Vanzetti*. Upton Sinclair wrote a novel called *Boston*, which concerned itself with the injustices of the trial of Sacco and Vanzetti. In 2001, Opera Tampa of Tampa Bay, Florida, presented *Sacco*

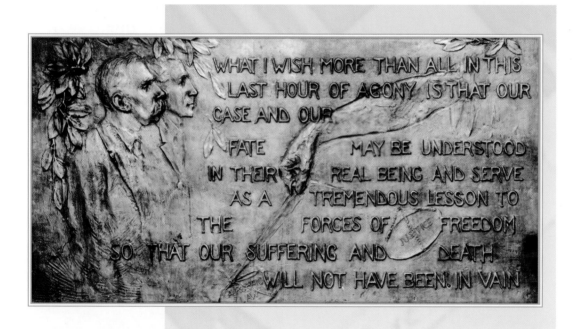

Sacco and Vanzetti are the subjects of this 1937 bas-relief by sculptor Gutzon Borglum. The plaque was initially refused by Massachusetts governor Charles F. Hurley, but was accepted forty-two years later by the Boston Public Library as part of the Felicani Sacco-Vanzetti Collection. Although the controversial trial still incites passionate arguments for both sides, it is possible that the legacy of Sacco and Vanzetti is stronger than the facts of their story. Innocent or guilty, the two men have a firm place in history as martyrs.

and Vanzetti, a two-act opera that was sung in the same Italian dialect that the two men would have used.

The state of Massachusetts made great strides in acknowledging the mistakes made during the trial and appeals process. In 1979, the Boston Public Library accepted the Felicani Sacco-Vanzetti Collection, which is one of the major sources of information on the lives, trials, and death of these two men. Two years prior, Governor Michael Dukakis proclaimed August 23 to be Sacco and Vanzetti Day. This was a major milestone and a real attempt to clear the names of these two men.

To this day, the case of Sacco and Vanzetti is still discussed at length. New evidence has been discovered since 1927. Many historians now believe that Sacco may have indeed been at the crime scene in South Braintree, but there has been no definitive evidence to support this theory. No matter how much new evidence or documentation is discovered, however, it should be remembered that Sacco and Vanzetti and their ordeal marked a significant point in American history—the tarnishing of the American Dream.

GLOSSARY

acquit To clear from a charge.

alibi An explanation for having been somewhere other than where a crime was committed that would make it impossible for the accused to have committed the crime.

allegation A statement made without proof.

anarchy A political movement that calls for the abolition of a formal government, relying only on self-rule.

appeal A request for a new hearing.

ballistics The science of how firearms function, and the study of the firing, flight, and effects of ammunition.

civil liberties Basic rights such as freedom of religion and free speech.

clemency An act of mercy.

communism A system of government in which a central organization governs the state and economy, with all produced goods shared by the people.

comrade A fellow member of a group who shares one's interests or activities.

defense The lawyer or team of lawyers representing the accused.

deliberate To consider all of the facts, testimony, and evidence before reaching a verdict.

indict To formally charge with a crime.

liberty Freedom.

prosecution The lawyer or team of lawyers whose goal is to convict the accused.

radical A person who favors large changes in an institution such as a government.

sedition Language or behavior that is intended to resist or rebel against a government or state.

socialism A political system that supports collective ownership and use of goods to form an equal society.

unbiased Being fair and without prejudice.

FOR MORE INFORMATION

Boston Public Library
Felicani Sacco-Vanzetti Collection
700 Boylston Street
Boston, MA 02117
(617) 536-5400
Web site: http://www.bpl.org

WEB SITES

Due to the changing nature of Internet links, the Rosen Publishing Group, Inc., has developed an online list of Web sites related to the subject of this book. This site is updated regularly. Please use this link to access the list:

http://www.rosenlinks.com/gttc/trsv

FOR FURTHER READING

Avrich, Paul. *Sacco and Vanzetti: The Anarchist Background*. Princeton, NJ: Princeton University Press, 1991.

Ehrmann, Herbert B. *The Case That Will Not Die: Commonwealth of Massachusetts vs. Nicola Sacco and Bartolomeo Vanzetti*. New York: Watts, 1969.

Fast, Howard. *The Passion of Sacco and Vanzetti: A New England Legend*. Westport, CT: Greenwood Press, 1972.

Frankfurter, Mary Denham, ed. *The Letters of Sacco and Vanzetti*. New York: Penguin, 1977.

Jackson, Brian. *The Black Flag: A Look Back at the Strange Case of Nicola Sacco and Bartolomeo Vanzetti*. Boston: Routledge & Kegan Paul, 1981.

Lee, Henry. *Famous Crimes Revisited: From Sacco-Vanzetti to O. J. Simpson*. Avon, CT: Publishing Directions, 2001.

Montgomery, Robert H. *Sacco-Vanzetti: The Murder and the Myth*. New York: Devin-Adair Company, 1960.

Young, William. *Postmortem: New Evidence in the Case of Sacco and Vanzetti*. Amherst, MA: University of Massachusetts Press, 1985.

BIBLIOGRAPHY

Felix, David. *Protest: Sacco-Vanzetti and the Intellectuals.* Bloomington, IN: Indiana University Press, 1965.

Feuerlicht, Roberta Strauss. *Justice Crucified: The Story of Sacco and Vanzetti.* New York: McGraw-Hill, 1977.

Frankfurter, Felix. *The Case of Sacco and Vanzetti: A Critical Analysis for Lawyers and Laymen.* New York: Universal Library, 1962.

Joughin, Louis, and Edmund M. Morgan. *The Legacy of Sacco and Vanzetti.* Chicago: Quadrangle Books, 1948.

Russell, Francis. *Sacco and Vanzetti: The Case Resolved.* New York: Harper & Row, 1986.

PRIMARY SOURCE IMAGE LIST

Cover: Photograph of Sacco and Vanzetti arriving at court. Taken in Dedham, Massachusetts, on April 19, 1927.

Page 4: Photograph of crowd protesting the Sacco and Vanzetti verdict. Taken in New York City on August 9, 1927.

Page 8: Photograph of Nicola, Dante, and Rosina Sacco. Taken around 1915, in Massachusetts.

Page 9: Photograph of Bartolomeo Vanzetti, taken in a Massachusetts courthouse in 1921.

Page 10: Political cartoon of the Statue of Liberty being brought down. Drawn by C. J. Taylor on October 27, 1886.

Page 15: Photograph of the Slater and Morrill shoe factory and the Rice and Hutchins factory. Taken in Braintree, Massachusetts, by John L. Farley. From the Massachusetts Supreme Judicial Court.

Page 16: Photograph of Sacco and Vanzetti's guns. From the Massachusetts Supreme Judicial Court.

Page 17: Photograph of Luigi Galleani.

Page 19: Photograph of Bullet 3. Taken by Wilbur F. Turner. From the Massachusetts Supreme Judicial Court.

Page 22: Photograph of the aftermath of a bomb explosion in New York City. Taken on September 16, 1920.

Page 23: Photograph of A. Mitchell Palmer in the Supreme Court. Taken in 1920 in Washington, D.C.

Page 24: Photographs of Nicola Sacco and Bartolomeo Vanzetti.

Page 29: Photograph of Judge Webster Thayer. From the Commonwealth Museum of Massachusetts.

Page 30: Cartoon, "Is This the Emblem?" drawn by Fred Ellis for the *Daily Worker* in 1927. Housed in the Michigan State University Library Special Collections Division.

Page 33: Photograph of police guarding courthouse in Dedham, Massachusetts. Taken on October 31, 1921.

Page 34: Photograph portrait of Fred Moore. Taken in 1927.

Page 35: Fund-raising petition for the defense of Sacco and Vanzetti. Created in 1921 by the Sacco-Vanzetti Defense Committee. Housed in the Chicago Federation of Labor Rights Collection, Chicago Historical Society.

Page 36: Photograph of Herbert Ehrmann and William Thompson. Taken in Boston, Massachusetts, in 1927.

Page 39: Photograph of a Buick automobile. Taken behind the Massachusetts statehouse by John L. Farley. From the Massachusetts Supreme Judicial Court.

Page 43: Photograph of Bartolomeo Vanzetti and Nicola Sacco. Taken in Dedham, Massachusetts, in 1921.

Page 46: Photograph of protesters rallying for Sacco and Vanzetti. Taken in 1927 in London, England.

Page 49: Photograph of Governor Alvan T. Fuller. Taken in his office in Massachusetts.

Page 50: Death masks and ashes of Sacco and Vanzetti. Created in August 1927 in Boston, Massachusetts. Photograph of the display taken by an Associated Press photographer on December 22, 1999, at the Boston Public Library.

Page 53: Photograph of the Sacco and Vanzetti funeral procession. Taken on August 26, 1927, in Boston, Massachusetts.

Page 54: Bas-relief of Sacco and Vanzetti. Sculpted by Gutzon Borglum in 1937. Housed in the Boston Public Library's Felicani Sacco-Vanzetti Collection.

INDEX

ABOUT THE AUTHOR

Kerry Hinton is a writer who lives in Hoboken, New Jersey.

CREDITS

Cover, pp. 1, 8, 9, 22 (inset), 23, 24, 34, 36, 43, 46, 49, 53 © Bettmann/Corbis; pp. 4, 33 © Underwood & Underwood/Corbis; pp. 10, 22 (left) © Corbis; pp. 15, 16, 19, 39 courtesy of the Massachusetts Supreme Judicial Court, division of Archives and Records Preservation, Boston; p. 17 courtesy of flag.blackened.net; p. 30 Michigan State University Library, Special Collections Division; p. 29 courtesy of the Commonwealth Museum at the Massachusetts Archives; p. 35 Chicago Historical Society; p. 50 © AP/Wide World Photos; p. 54 by courtesy of the Trustees of the Boston Public Library.

ACKNOWLEDGMENTS

The publisher would like to thank Stephen Kenney, director of the Commonwealth Museum at the Massachusetts Archives, and Elizabeth Bouvier, head of archives for the Massachusetts Supreme Judicial Court, for their help with some of the photos in this book.

Designer: Les Kanturek; **Editor:** Christine Poolos